The World's Best Gambling Jokes

The World's Best Gambling Jokes

Graham Sharpe

Illustrated by Graham Morris

Fontana
An Imprint of HarperCollins*Publishers*

Fontana
An Imprint of HarperCollins*Publishers*,
77–85 Fulham Palace Road,
Hammersmith, London W6 8JB

A Fontana Original 1992

9 8 7 6 5 4 3 2 1

A catalogue record for this book is
available from the British Library

ISBN 0 00 637808 0

Set in Linotron Goudy Old Style by
Falcon Typographic Art Ltd, Edinburgh

Printed and bound in Great Britain by
BPCC Hazells Ltd
Member of BPCC Ltd

The
World's Best
Gambling
Jokes

REALLY IN THE RUNNING

The punter at the big meeting had staked £1000 on the first five losers of the day, but he told the bookie he didn't really mind as long as he heard his horse mentioned in the commentary and got a run for his money.

When the punter doubled his stake to back a 100/1 outsider, Bill's Boy, in the last race, Harry the bookie, not wishing to lose such a good customer, had a word in the ear of the racecourse commentator, asking him to give the no-hoper at least a mention or two.

As the field came to the last fence the commentator said 'With one to jump, Bill's Boy has leapt to the front and gone three lengths clear – and I'm not ----ing joking, Harry.'

STONE ME!

Two archaeologists were digging out in the desert when they came across ancient human remains. After a swift examination one turned to the other and said, 'This man definitely committed suicide.'

'How can you tell?' asked his companion.

'Well, he has a note clutched in his hand. It says 5000 shekels win Goliath!'

BORN LOSER

Then there was the gambling burglar who broke into a betting shop – and lost £100.

WAYNE OUT IN FRONT

Two friends were on their way to see a John Wayne movie. One bet the other £50 that Wayne would fall off his horse at the end of the film. He did, and the winner, accepting the cash, said: 'Actually I knew I'd win – I've seen the film before.' The other replied: 'So have I – but I didn't think he'd be so stupid as to fall off again.'

HARE TODAY

The novice punter was studying the card for a greyhound race when another punter advised him, 'Back the hare, it always wins.'

'Back the hare?' said the novice. 'Surely you can't do that.'

'Yes, you can – just ask the bookie.'

The novice went up to the counter and asked the bookie for £10 on the hare which was duly accepted.

After the race he went back for his winnings, only to be told:

'You know the hare won, the hare knows it won, I know it won – but that bloody stupid judge has gone and given it to trap five!'

The punter was so ecstatic at having backed a winner that he rushed into the Winner's Enclosure and planted a huge, smacking kiss on the horse which had just brought about such a dramatic increase in his fortunes.

This gesture was not well received by the horse's snooty owner, who looked down his nose at the punter, called for security men to have him chucked out and said: 'I say, what

damnably bad behaviour, you oik! How dare you do that to my horse!'

The quick-thinking punter replied, 'Terribly sorry, old boy, I thought it was your wife!'

The Monarch of the country and one of his loyal subjects were playing a game of poker. The bidding was fast and furious and there was a large sum of money in the pot when the royal player finally demanded to see his opponent's hand.

The loyal subject turned over four queens.

The Monarch laid down three kings and made to pick up the money.

'Excuse me, sire, but I fear you have lost,' ventured the subject apprehensively.

'But how do you come to that conclusion?' roared His Highness.

'Well, sire, I have four queens – you have but three kings.'

'Nonsense,' declared the Monarch, collecting in the cash. 'I have four kings – those three, plus myself.'

What do you have when you have ten bookmakers buried up to their necks in sand?
Not enough sand.

What's a bookmaker's favourite time of day? – 25/1 (twenty-five to one).

Then there was the roulette player who sent a telegram home: 'System working well – send more money.'

Charles Greville, famous diarist, and owner of 1837 St Leger winner, Mango, wrote in 1838: 'Racing is just like dram drinking; momentary excitement and wretched intervals; full consciousness of the mischievous effects of the habit and equal difficulty in abstaining from it.'

GAMBLING BOOKS

The Unluckiest Punter by Mr Winner
Failed Systems by I.O. Yew
Never Trust a Tipster by R.U. Shaw
Successful Betting by Honour Winna
Bluffing at Cards by King Hi
Craps Dice by Raoul A. Severn
Be a Croupier by Turner V. Kards
The Winning Streak by E. Zee Munny
How to Avoid Gambling Conmen by B.A.Ware
Bingo Made Easy by Howe C. Howzee
How to Gamble by Bet Wright
Beating the Bookies by Noah Chance
Making Poker Pay by Cardew Choose
The Evils of Gambling by Cardinal Syn

The excited racehorse owner rushed into his local betting shop and demanded to see the manager, telling him, 'I have just "seen" my horse win next Saturday's Grand National in a dream.'

'Oh yeah?' said the bookie. 'I suggest you wake up quickly then – the thing's a 500/1 outsider – it couldn't win if it started now.'

'No, it was a sign, I saw everything clearly, right down to

the black armband the jockey was wearing. I saw them jump Becher's and I saw my horse go clear on the run in to win by ten lengths. I *must* back him – put £1000 on for me!'

'Well, it's your money, if you want to chuck it away . . .' said the bookie.

Grand National Day came. The race went precisely as the owner had dreamed: his horse soared over Becher's Brook, ran brilliantly and stormed away on the run in to win by ten lengths. The jockey even wore a black armband.

Which explains why the owner never collected his winnings.

He died the day before.

The famous footballer who had played around with women, boozed and gambled his career away, was returning to his hotel room after a night on the town with his latest girlfriend, a former Miss World.

They stumbled through the door and flopped down on the bed. The footballer emptied his pockets of bundles of fivers which he'd won in the casino that night and rang room service demanding to be sent up two bottles of the best champagne in the place. Meanwhile, his girlfriend stripped down to her frilly lingerie and lay on the bed.

They were just beginning to make love when there was a knock on the door.

'Come in,' called the soccer star.

The porter pushed open the door, wheeling in a trolley on which was a solid silver ice bucket containing two bottles of the finest champagne and looked at the two on the bed. ''Ere, I know you, don't I, mate. Yeah, you used to play for Manchester United, didn't you?'

'Yes,' confirmed the footballer player.

The porter looked around him – at the superb champagne, at the unclad beauty, at the hundreds of pounds of gambling winnings.

'God! How did it all go wrong!'

A hare, dressed in a Nike running vest, Reebok running shorts and Hi-Tec running shoes walked into a betting shop. He jogged up to the counter and told the manager, 'Put me a grand on the tortoise.'

T he jockey dismounted from the horse, which had lost the race because of his tendency to hang to the right in the final furlong.

'What should I do about it?' the trainer asked the jockey.

'Put a bit of lead in his left ear,' the jockey answered.

'How can I do that?' asked the trainer.

'With a bloody shotgun!'

H onest Joe had a customer who regularly backed long-priced winners and made a good living out of the game.

When Honest Joe died suddenly his partner, Long Odds Fred, took over his business, and with it the business of Jim, the lucky punter.

Shortly after, Jim the punter fell ill and was rushed into hospital where it was discovered that he required urgent surgery.

Just before he was to carry out the life or death operation the surgeon came in to see Jim to ask him if he was prepared for the ordeal.

'I am,' said Jim, 'but could you do me a favour – ring up my bookie and tell him I want a grand on Foinavon in the National.'

'Certainly,' replied the surgeon and he went off to phone Long Odds Fred as requested.

'This is the surgeon at the hospital. Jim the lucky punter is my patient, I am about to operate on him and I'm not so sure that he'll pull through. He's asked me to put £1000 on Foinavon for him in this afternoon's Grand National.'

'Oh, has he?' said Long Odds Fred. 'Then just you tell him to wait a couple of hours and put his bloody bet on with Honest Joe.'

Two bookies, or layers as they are known, met at the entrance to Ascot racecourse.

'You look a bit below par, Jack,' said Honest Al.

'Yeah, well, to tell the truth I've had a lot on my mind – I'm worried about this ozone layer business.'

'Oh, no need to worry about him, they won't give him a pitch here!'

The racecourse bookie was busy taking bets when all of a sudden one of the punters dropped dead in front of him.

The doctor was called, but there was nothing he could do.

'Well, we'll stop taking bets out of respect,' said the bookie. But two minutes later he was shouting the odds as loud as ever with the prostrate body still laid out in front of him awaiting the arrival of the ambulance.

'I thought you'd stopped taking bets out of respect,' said the doctor.

'And so we did,' said the bookie, 'but we only allow two minutes silence for the dead of two World Wars, for God's sake!'

T he inveterate racing punter finally died. He found himself standing at the pearly gates trying to gain entry past the resident 'Jobsworth', who was wearing a small bowler hat and standing next to a notice reading 'No jeans allowed'.

'Do you think I might come in?' asked the punter.

The gateman explained that heaven had just introduced a quota system – so many lawyers, so many doctors, so many grocers, so many racing people – and the quota of racegoers and punters had just been filled for the season.

'Well,' said the punter. 'If I can persuade somebody to leave, could I have his place?'

'Persuade someone to leave Heaven! No one's ever done that before. Mind you, there's no rule against it. I suppose you could have a try. Remember, though, you're on a twenty-four-hour pass and if you don't succeed, after that you'll have to come out and go to Hell, or Epsom as we call it.'

The punter shuddered and went in. He soon found the racing section and was greeted by ghosts, phantoms and spirits anxious for recent news of the racing scene. 'Oh, its much the same: Piggott's made another comeback, Pipe's trained five hundred winners, Claud Duval hasn't tipped a winner this season . . .'

Draining the last of his pint of ambrosia, the punter looked thoughtful and said, 'I did hear something on the way up, though – they're opening up a thirty-day meeting in Hell with guaranteed prize money of £50,000 for each race and

guaranteed betting of 10/1 the field in each race of eight runners or less.'

Suddenly, there was a great rushing of air as angels, spirits, cherubs, phantoms and ghosts made a sudden dash for the exit.

Laughing, the punter looked around him. 'That's me in, then. I suppose most of the others will be back soon and we can spend eternity discussing racing and gambling.'

But a week passed and no one had returned, so he wandered back to the pearly gate for a chat with the jobsworth.

'Any of the lads back yet?' he asked.

'Not one,' said the Jobsworth. 'They went out of here like bats out of Hell! It looks like you're safely in now.'

'Mm,' pondered the punter. 'You know, I reckon there just might have been something in that story I told them after all.'

There was a small rushing of air as the punter made a dash for the exit.

The racehorse owner rang his stable and asked whether the trainer could make sure the yard would be spotlessly clean at 10.30 the next morning as he was bringing a friend to look around.

Hoping to acquire more business, the trainer made his staff take extra care in cleaning the place up and sure enough at 10.30 the owner and another man arrived.

The owner led his smartly dressed companion around, pointing out the horses as he went.

The two stayed for half an hour then, thanking the trainer, they left.

Shortly after, as the trainer sat thinking to himself how

pleasant it would be to have another owner on the books, his head stable lad knocked on the office door and asked him exactly when four of the best horses in the yard had changed hands and been bought by the owner who had been showing his friend around the yard that morning.

Puzzled, the trainer told the lad that the horses hadn't changed hands at all. 'That's odd,' said the lad, 'only the owner was telling his friend that all four of them were his, as well as the one he really does own.'

The trainer forgot about the incident until later that evening when the owner rang him to ask about running plans for his horse.

'We've got him in a race at Newton Abbot – he should win,' said the trainer. 'By the way, is that friend of yours going to buy a horse and let me train it for him?'

'What?' said the owner. 'What makes you think he'll do that?'

'Wasn't he a prospective owner, then?'

'Of course not,' laughed the owner. 'Why do you think I told him I owned those four other good horses?'

'I've no idea.'

'Well, he's my bank manager, and it's a hell of a lot easier to get a bigger overdraft when he thinks I've got five bloody good horses in training.'

Two members of the landed gentry had been out for a day's shooting on Lord X's estate.

Before setting off, Lord X and his guest, Lord Y, had wagered a substantial amount as to which of them would shoot the heaviest 'bag'.

With time running out the two were neck and neck and the

impecunious Lord Y was extremely concerned that he was about to be landed with a debt which he could not meet.

As the two 'weighed in' it seemed that Lord X would come out on top.

Lord Y looked desperately around him for a way out of his plight. Inspiration suddenly struck, he took careful aim with his gun – and shot the host's pointer bitch.

STONE COLD CERT

A man goes into the bookie's on Grand National Day with four pebbles, and demands to put it all on Red Rum. The manager laughs and tells the man he needs money to place a bet.

But the man insists he wants to stake the pebbles so, to humour him, the manager takes the pebbles and gives him a betting slip in return.

When Red Rum wins the man comes in to claim his winnings, so the manager tells his counter clerk to go out into the car park and fill a carrier bag full of gravel for him.

The man goes away delighted with his 'winnings' but shortly afterwards he returns with a large boulder which he puts on the counter.

The manager looks at him and says, 'Oh, no, you can get lost. You must have had a hot tip for one!'

The woman went into the casino with a fiver in her purse. She plunged it all on number twenty-one at the roulette table. Number twenty-one came up. She left the winnings there and it won again.

Her good fortune continued until she was over £100,000 up – then she ran out of luck and began losing. As she lost she

doubled up her stakes. Eventually she had lost the lot.

On her way home she saw a friend and told her where she'd been.

'How did you get on?' asked the friend.

'Lost a fiver,' she said.

A man with a stammer went into a betting shop and said to the manager, 'I've b-b-b-backed a f-f-five t-t-. . .'

'Five to one?' said the bookie.

'N-n-no,' said the stammerer, 'I've b-b-backed a f-f-five t-t-. . .'

'Five to two?' asked the bookie, trying to be helpful.

'N-n-no,' said the man. 'I-I-I've b-b-backed . . .'

Exasperated, the bookie said, 'Here, take this tenner, I'm busy at the moment, we'll settle up properly later.'

'Okay, th-th-thanks,' said the man and left. Outside, his mate said to him, 'What did you back?'

'I b-b-backed my f-f-five t-t-ton l-l-lorry into his c-c-car.'

Father and son came home after an afternoon trip.

'How did you enjoy the zoo, Johnny?' asked Mum.

'Oh, it was great – and Dad enjoyed it, too. Especially when one of the animals came racing home at 20/1.'

The jockey had been beaten on the 'good thing' – the owner was not amused.

'Why didn't you go for the gap?' he demanded of the rider.

'Well,' replied the bemused jockey. 'The gap was going faster than we were.'

The jockey and trainer were conferring after another 'good thing' had been beaten in a sprint race.

'Do you think he stays?' asked the trainer.

'Yes,' said the jockey. 'Too bloody long in the same place.'

Tom and Fred are crossing the racecourse on their way home after a day at the races during which they have lost all their money and enjoyed a few too many drinks.

It is becoming dark and the crowds have dispersed. As they begin to walk across, Fred grabs Tom's arm and rushes him to the other side of the track.

'What are you doing?' asked Tom.

'We've gotta be careful,' said Fred. 'That horse we backed in the last race – well, he's still running out here somewhere!'

The attractive girl was anxiously asking people on the racecourse, 'Could you please lend me a pin?'

As she asked one racegoer, someone behind her suddenly shouted out: 'They're off!'

The girl promptly fainted.

The hot favourite won the race in great style, but as the jockey pulled his mount up he was accidentally unseated and crashed to the ground.

He was badly injured and rushed to hospital.

After collecting the huge winnings he had received courtesy of the jockey, a punter decided to ring the hospital and check on the jockey's health.

He was put through to the ward.

'Excuse me, sister, can you tell me how the jockey who was brought in recently is getting on.'

'Isn't it obvious?' she asked.

'I beg your pardon?'

'Well, he's a jockey, isn't he?'

'Er, yes . . .'

'Then he's in a stable condition.'

An Irish trainer was heard to remark that the only time the Curragh trainers ever got together was for one another's funeral – and then it was to get the horses off the widow.

'I'm here to make a small fortune,' announced the flashy arrival at the casino.

'There's only one way you'll do that,' the pro gambler told him, 'and that's to start with a large one!'

The irate slot machine punter complained to the casino manager:

'Listen, I just dropped fifty dollars in that machine and only got back four quarters – don't these slot machines ever pay off?'

Replied the manager:

'Lady, they sure do: they pay the casino's rent, the light bills and all the casino employees' salaries plus a cool half a million dollars a year in profits – sure, they pay off.'

Then there was the trainer who prepared his charges on whisky, brandy and rum. 'They may not be the best racehorses in the world, but they're certainly the bloody happiest,' he was heard to comment.

The poker player thought he was on to a sure winner when a grizzled old timer sat down to play against him.

But the old timer parted the player from his cash so quickly that he accused him of cheating.

'Look, my friend,' said the old timer, 'I beat you because you don't know the first thing about gambling. Would you bet $500 right now against me taking my right eye out and laying it on the table?'

The player was taken aback. He had seen the old timer's play and knew that he was a first-rate bluffer. This, he thought, must be more of the same. But here was his chance to recoup some of his losses.

'Sure,' he said excitedly, reaching for his wallet and throwing five $100 bills down.

The old timer covered the bet, took out his glass eye, placed it on the table and scooped up the money.

'And now,' he said, 'will you bet me $1000 that I can't take the other one out?'

The poker player, by now totally bemused, shook his head and refused the bet, only later realizing that he must have refused the greatest certainty of all time.

The card sharp walked into the saloon, looking for easy pickings.

He spotted four grizzly prospectors playing poker.

'Is this game open to all comers?' he asked them. He was invited to sit down.

After playing fairly for an hour or so to lull his opponents, the card sharp stacked the cards, dealing himself four aces.

He made a large bet and one of the prospectors dropped

out, another large bet and another dropped out. By the time there was just the card sharp and one prospector left in the game there was a tidy sum on the table.

The prospector called the card sharp who showed his four aces and made to collect up the cash.

'Not so fast, sonny,' said the prospector, laying down his cards – the three, five and seven of clubs plus the eight and ten of diamonds.

'What do you mean?' asked the card sharp. 'I've got four aces.'

'So you have,' was the reply. 'But in this here town a Lollapalooza beats any other hand. And that's what I've got – three clubs and two diamonds.'

The other prospectors nodded in agreement. 'That's right, stranger. Nothing beats a Lollapalooza.'

The card sharp realized he had been conned, but figured he would get his own back. On his next deal he stacked the cards again, this time dealing himself a Lollapalooza hand and giving four aces to the prospector who had beaten him.

Once again the betting was fast and furious, building up to a hefty pot when just the two of them were left in.

Once again the prospector called the card sharp, who triumphantly showed his hand, grinning, 'This time I can't lose. I've got a Lollapalooza.'

'Sorry, partner,' said the prospector, raking in the pot. 'You should ask about the rules before you sit down to play – the Lollapalooza hand can only be played once a night.'

An elderly, distinguished looking gentleman, looking ever so slightly the worse for drink was weaving unsteadily through the players in the casino, loudly bemoaning his own misfortune and complaining that he must be the unluckiest punter alive.

'What do you mean, unlucky?' asked the croupier.

'Well, number twenty-seven won, didn't it?' said the drunk.

'Yes, but you didn't put a bet on it. What's unlucky about that?' asked the croupier.

'But I did have a bet; I had a bet in my own mind. I was going to put £20 on number twenty-six – and I lost. Here, take this, I always settle my debts.' And the drunk forced a twenty-pound note on the croupier.

The croupier tried to return the money, but the drunk insisted he should accept it so, finally, the croupier shrugged and banked the money.

The drunk weaved away, apparently heading towards the bar – but a few minutes later he was back.

He walked up to the table just as the croupier spun the ball, watched until the ball dropped into number fourteen then began to shout loudly: 'Yes, that's my number – yes, I bet twenty pounds on number fourteen and it's come up.'

The croupier looked at him: 'I'm sorry, sir, you didn't place a bet.'

'Oh yes I did,' announced the 'drunk', now stone cold sober. 'I had a bet in my own mind – and I won. You took my money when I lost – now you owe me £700.'

The croupier had to pay.

Leading poker player Eric Drache was delighted when the prestigious *Gambling Times* named him the sixth best Seven Card Stud player in the world, until he read the next line of the story: 'Drache's trouble is that he only plays with the top five.'

Famous German philosopher Arthur Schopenhauer used to take meals at an inn frequented by English military personnel.

At the start of each meal he placed a gold coin in front of him; at the end of the meal he would pick it up and pocket it.

Finally, a waiter asked the meaning of this ritual.

Schopenhauer told the waiter that he had a wager with himself each day: he would lose the wager and place the coin in the poor box on the day the English officers spoke of anything other than horses, dogs or women.

A friend spotted French dramatist Tristan Bernard (1866–1947) walking along the promenade at Deauville wearing a new yachting cap.

When the friend passed a complimentary remark about the cap Bernard told him he had just bought it with his winnings from the previous night's play at the casino.

The friend congratulated him.

'But,' added Bernard, 'what I lost would have bought me the yacht!'

Actor and racehorse owner Wilfrid Hyde-White was making an unfortunate appearance in the bankruptcy court. During the course of his cross-examination the official receiver commented: 'Mr Hyde-White, if you cannot tell us how you spent such a large sum in so short a time, perhaps you could tell us what will win the Gold Cup at Ascot this afternoon?'

'Of course, dear fellow,' replied Hyde-White, naming the horse which did, in fact, win the race. 'But only have a small bet – we don't want to have to change places, do we?'

Gordon Richards, the world famous jockey, was about to receive his knighthood. As the monarch stepped forward to perform the ceremony, Richards commented: 'I've always wanted to be known as the shortest knight of the year.'

American movie producer Harry Cohn, head of Columbia Studios, was asked by his brother Jack whether they should produce a biblical epic.

'What do you know about the Bible?' demanded Harry. 'I'll bet fifty dollars you don't even know the Lord's Prayer.'

After a moment's thought Jack began, 'Now I lay me down to sleep . . .'

Harry counted out fifty dollars and handed it to his brother: 'Well, I'll be damned, I didn't think you knew it.'

A lady once sat next to Calvin Coolidge, thirtieth President of the United States (1923–29), and told him, 'I have made a bet, Mr Coolidge, that I can get more than two words out of you.'

Said Coolidge: 'You lose.'

French actor Lucien Guitry (1860–1925) was once sent the manuscript of a play by a fellow thespian who attached a note to it saying, 'I'll bet you a louis that you don't read this script.'

Guitry sent it straight back, unopened – attached to it was a louis and a note saying, 'You win.'

John Heidegger, manager of the Opera House at London's Haymarket in the early eighteenth century was very proud of his own ugliness. He once bet Lord Chesterfield that the latter could not find anyone uglier.

Chesterfield produced a hideous old woman, and claimed his winnings.

Heidegger promptly removed her bonnet, perched it on his own head, and was adjudged the winner.

Mozart is said to have wagered fellow composer Haydn that he could compose a piece which Haydn could not play. The stake was a case of champagne.

Mozart duly produced the piece; Haydn began to play on the piano.

He played the first few bars easily before coming to a dead stop when confronted with an instruction to play with two hands at either end of the keyboard and, simultaneously, play a note in the centre.

Haydn admitted defeat and Mozart stepped forward to the keyboard, placed a hand at either end, then bent forward and played the middle note – with his nose.

The elderly stranger in the pub watched the locals playing darts.

'I've never seen a dartboard before,' he told them. 'But it looks an interesting game. If you explain the rules I'll play you for a few quid.'

A few explanations later the stranger had clearly got the message and he quickly cleaned the locals out.

Disgruntled they asked him, 'How come you said you were new to darts?'

'No, I said new to the dartboard. I was a prisoner of war for three years and all we had was a set of darts. I used to practise by pinning flies to the wall of the hut.'

'Surely the blood made a bit of a mess?'

'Not when you pinned 'em by one leg.'

The raffle organizer sold two tickets to his pal in the pub who told him, 'I'll pay you later.'

Next day the organizer was back in the pub.

'Who won the raffle?' asked his mate.

'I did, aren't I lucky?'

'Who won second prize?'

'My wife, wasn't she lucky?'

'Who won third prize?'

'My son, wasn't he lucky? By the way, you didn't pay me for your tickets.'

'No, aren't I lucky?'

The Irish priest was stopping passers-by to ask for directions to the church in an unfamiliar town.

'Well, you turn right at the Red Lion, left at the White

Horse, left again at the Railway Hotel then you can't miss it.'

The priest looked bemused. He obviously had no idea that these were pub names, and tried another passer-by.

'Go past Our Price, along as far as Next, up the road to the disco and it's just down the road.'

More blank looks – he tried again.

'Well, Father, you go down as far as the Mecca, turn left, go along to the Ladbrokes, right there as far as Corals, left, then along to William Hill and it's on the corner opposite.'

'T'ank God ye came along, m'son. Oi'd never have found it otherwise.'

T he alien was reporting back to the Supreme Master of his spaceship following a flying visit to Earth.

'I visited a gathering of female earthlings in what is clearly some kind of holy shrine.

'They all sit quietly in rows in a large hall. Each earthling has a number of small cards in front of her. A male earthling sits on an elevated platform constantly calling out numbers to which the earthlings listen with rapt attention.

'At the height of the ceremony the male utters a number which obviously has religious significance. At this one female shouts at the top of her voice the utterance *Bingo* and the rest of the assembled multitude reply, *Oh shit.*'

ONE LINERS . . .

A racehorse is the only creature which can take thousands of people for a ride at the same time . . .

A horse is something that can run like hell until you bet a tenner that he can . . .

I bet on a horse that got a ticket for parking . . .

My bookie and I have a Siamese twin relationship – we're joined at the wallet . . .

In horse racing there's nothing so uncertain as a sure thing . . .

The two crooked tipsters met during a race meeting.

One told the other, 'I've found a great punter – he's loaded and he's been putting a hundred quid for me on every tip I've given him. The only trouble is they've all got beat. He's had five losers in a row. What do you reckon I should do now?'

'Give him up,' said the other. 'He's bad luck.'

The two gamblers met up – one looking very smart in a brand new suit.

'I got it by backing a horse,' he told his mate.

'Oh, where?'

'Through Burton's window.'

The gambler stood up in the crowded casino:

'Anyone lost a roll of fivers with a rubber band around them?'

A stampede of other gamblers headed for him. First to arrive was an elderly gent, to whom the gambler said, 'Here, I've found your rubber band.'

A racehorse walked up to the on-course bookie and asked for a tenner on himself.

The bookie looked amazed.

'What's the matter?' said the horse. 'Haven't you ever heard of a talking horse?'

'It's not that. I just can't believe you think you can win!'

A man walking along the road on his way to the betting shop saw a horse looking over a hedge. As he passed by the horse it said to him, 'Did you know I won the Grand National twelve years ago?'

The man was so shocked that he rushed straight into the nearest pub and ordered a large scotch, telling the barman that he'd just had a nasty shock.

'Don't tell me, that horse out there has been speaking to you?' said the barman.

'Yes,' replied the man, amazed.

'What did he say?' asked the barman.

'He told me he won the National twelve years ago.'

'Hmm, bloody typical. He's a liar, he was only second.'

In the days before photo finishes two horses came to the finishing line virtually together. Although it was tight, jockey Brown was convinced he'd won, only for the judge to place him second.

In the next race, Brown came to the line a fence clear of his opponents, stood up in the stirrups and shouted, 'Oy, you bastard, it's me again! Can you bloody well see me this time?'

The judge saw him all right, and heard him, and suspended him for abusive conduct.

The old lady walked into the betting shop to place her bet.

'Do you want it each way?' asked the counter clerk.

'Each way? Do I have to back it going to the start as well as coming back?'

The competitive bookie would never be outdone. If the bookie next to him offered 2/1, he would quote 9/4. If the opposition went 3/1 he had to be 7/2.

Then the bookie took up golf. Seeing him out on the course one day an acquaintance asked his partner how the bookie was getting on.

'Not bad,' he said. 'But there's just one snag – we can't get him to shout "Fore" – it has to be "Nine to two"!'

Wilson Mizner (1876–1933), an American writer and wit, was playing poker with an opponent who suddenly pulled out his wallet and tossed it on the table.

Mizner calmly took off a shoe, put it on the table and said, 'If we're playing for leather, I raise you.'

Mizner was enjoying a cruise, one of whose diversions was a daily lottery in which passengers guessed at the number of miles covered by the ship during a twenty-four-hour period.

Mizner decided to give luck a helping hand and targeted

an officer with access to the ship's log who, Mizner thought, might be prepared to 'go bent'.

Standing outside the officer's cabin, Mizner announced very loudly the number he had drawn in the lottery and added: 'You know what I'd do if I won? I'd stick a thousand dollars under the right officer's pillow.'

When the winning lottery number was announced it was Mizner's.

By bringing an accomplice into the game Mizner also managed to win the next day's lottery in the same way.

On the third day they cleaned up again. But on the fourth, as they took up position outside the cabin door, a voice growled at them: 'Clear off, you bastards, I'm four hundred miles off course already.'

American writer Franklin Adams (1881–1960) belonged to a poker club which boasted amongst its members a certain actor, Herbert Ransom, whose hands could easily be deduced by his facial grimaces.

Adams proposed a club rule that 'Anyone who looks at Ransom's face is cheating.'

The jockey had just returned from his first meeting in France.

'How did you get on with the snails?' asked his friend.

'Well, I didn't eat any but I certainly rode a few.'

The boxer had taken a pasting.

He was carried from the ring back to his dressing room.

The medic arrived.

'I feel pretty bad, Doc,' said the pug.

'Not half as bad as I do, I had a grand on you to win,' the doc said.

The punter had been given a very hot tip by a trainer, 'Back my horse called Lunch, it won't be beaten.'

The next day the punter decided to go and back the horse, but he called in at the pub on the way for a swift half.

Eight pints later he was well away when all of a sudden he remembered the bet, but he'd forgotten the name of the horse.

He looked up and spotted a sign: 'Lunch, 12–1'.

That was it! He said to the barman, 'Can you get me a tenner on that horse there, Lunch, at 12–1?'

The barman, assuming he'd had one too many, chucked the punter out. He staggered into the next pub, where he saw a sign: 'Lunch, 11–2'.

'Oh, no, they're backing it and I've missed the price,' he said, frantically calling the barman over and demanding that he be laid the 12–1.

He was chucked out again.

Into the next pub he tottered, only to see 'Lunch 1–2'.

'Oh shit, I'm not going to back an odds-on chance,' he said.

Just then a waitress emerged, holding a plate and calling 'Sausages, one!'

'Great, it lost! Thank God I didn't get on,' sighed the punter.

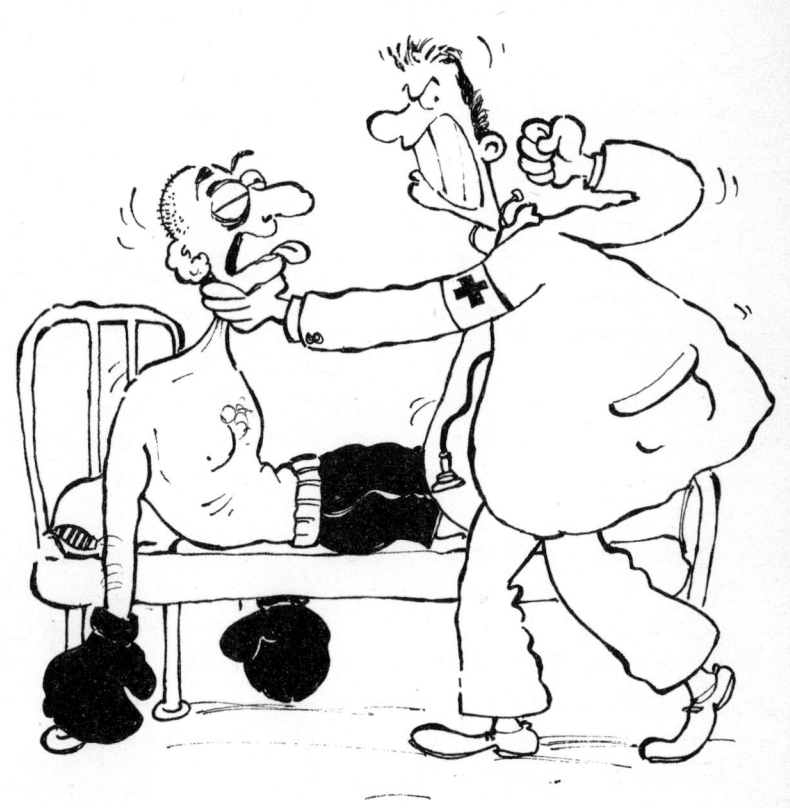

'Treat this horse gently,' said the trainer to the jockey. 'Give her an easy race, bring her in fourth.'

The jockey duly carried out the instructions, bringing the horse in fourth out of twelve.

'Do you think you'll beat the three in front next time out?' asked the trainer.

'Certainly,' said the jockey, 'but I wouldn't be so sure about the eight behind.'

The two Jewish punters met on the way home from the races.

Hymie had backed four long-odds winners. Abie had backed only losers.

'So tell me how you do it?' said Abie to Hymie.

'It's very simple. Before I go to the track I go and pray in the synagogue and I never fail to back four winners a day.'

Abie, whose adherence to his religion had lapsed somewhat decided he had nothing to lose.

Off he went to the synagogue. After an hour's hard praying he went off to the track. Every bet he made was a loser.

On the way home he saw Hymie.

'So how did you do?' asked Hymie, 'I backed four more winners.'

'No good, I backed all losers once more,' complained Abie.

'But didn't you take my advice and pray in the synagogue?' said Hymie.

'Yes, I did – but, nothing.'

Said Hymie, 'I can't understand it. Tell me, what synagogue did you pray in?'

'Well,' said Abie, 'the one in Golders Green, of course.'

'Oy veh,' said Hymie, 'Golders Green! Well, you schmo, didn't you know that Golders Green is for the greyhounds?'

A born loser, the gambler finally realized his luck wasn't about to change, and packed in betting.

Some months later a pal told him he had an absolute certainty.

Against his better judgement the born loser decided to give it one more try, so he drew out a hundred quid from his bank account and went down to the betting shop to back the tip.

He waited for the commentary of the race in which his horse, Blackie, a 20/1 shot was running. It was a steeplechase and as the race progressed the commentator suddenly said:

'There's a fog coming down here and with two to jump the favourite is in front but Blackie's gaining on him and challenging strongly . . . now they've gone into the mist and I can't pick them out . . . now they're out of the fog and approaching the last, it's the favourite and Blackie together . . . and as they come to the last they've disappeared back into thick fog and, yes, one of them's fallen, but I can't tell which one . . .'

At this point the born loser jumped to his feet and bellowed,

'That bloody commentator, he's only a couple of hundred yards away from the race and he can't make out which horse fell. Me, I'm a couple of hundred *miles* away – and I bloody well *know* which bloody horse fell!'

A horse called Coffee suddenly attracted some huge bets just before the race was about to start. It was backed down from 16/1 to 4/1 and having just taken some stiff wagers for it the bookie decided he'd have to lay off some of his liabilities.

'Quick, go and get 4s Coffee,' he ordered his clerk, handing him a wad of notes.

The clerk decided to take a chance and keep the cash, hoping that the horse would lose.

Coffee stormed home by ten lengths.

In desperate trouble now, the clerk thought quickly and walked back to the bookie's stand with four cups of tea on a tray. As the bemused bookie stared at him the clerk said, 'Sorry, they'd run out of coffee so I got four teas instead, here's your change.'

The Irish trainer was celebrating his horse's victory in a £500 handicap event when his pal congratulated him, saying,

'The way he won that race you ought to enter him for the Grand National.'

'What do you take me for – if he went and won the Grand National what sort of weight d'you reckon he'd get in this race next season.'

The trainer was bringing his top horse down from Scotland for a race at Newton Abbot in which the horse was due to land a big gambling coup. He decided to drive down the day before but got lost and decided he would have to find somewhere to spend the night before continuing the journey the next morning.

He pulled up at a farmhouse, explained the situation and

asked whether he could stay and whether the farmer could put his horse, a mare, in his barn.

'Well, my stallion is kept in there and he's a right randy bugger,' said the farmer.

'That's okay, I'll cover my mare with a sheet, she'll be all right.'

Next morning the trainer went to fetch his mare, only to find the barn door hanging off its hinges. The stallion stood inside looking happy with himself, but there was no sign of the mare.

The trainer set off down the nearest road, asking everyone he met, 'Have you seen a horse covered with a white sheet anywhere around?'

No one had, until he came across an old boy leaning over a gate shaking his head.

'Excuse me, sir, I'm looking for a horse of mine, she was covered in a white sheet and I think she may have come this way.'

'No, sir,' said the old boy, 'I ain't seen no horse in a white sheet, but a while back I did see some horse come hurtling past here with an 'andkerchief shoved up its arse.'

The new steward was out with a more experienced colleague watching a race.

As the horses finished the race they both noticed one being tenderly ridden, the jockey obviously not making any serious attempt to win.

'Did you see that?' asked the new steward.

'Hmm, yes,' said his colleague.

'What do you intend to do about it?'

'Back it next time out, of course.'

The owner arrived at the stables unexpectedly to see his horse.

Unbeknown to the owner, the horse had fallen ill and the trainer had had it shot three weeks previously, but he hadn't told the owner, hoping to be able to charge him for looking after the horse for as long as he could.

'Well, why on earth didn't you tell me?' demanded the owner, once he had discovered the truth.

'I saved you three weeks training fees as it was, do you mean to say you expected me to waste the cost of a first-class stamp as well?'

The Italian jockey hired to ride the British owner's horse in the Italian Derby had ridden a hopeless race and the horse was well beaten.

When the translator asked the owner if he wanted to say anything to the jockey the distraught owner bellowed 'Tell him he's a c··t and he makes me scream', little believing that this message would be passed on.

To the owner's great surprise the translator actually began to pass on the message – but the jockey smiled and nodded his head.

'Excuse me,' said the owner to the translator, 'what did you tell the jockey I said?'

'Just-a what you told-a me,' said the translator. 'That his-a country make-a a great ice-a cream.'

The wealthy racehorse owner was always seen at the races with a glamorous-looking tart at his side.

One day he arrived on his own to watch one of his horses run.

'And where is your lady friend?' he was asked.

'I had to make up my mind between her and my horses – and her entry fees were higher.'

The keen punter was relaxing on his day off with a round of golf.

After going round in a respectable eighty he was at the nineteenth hole enjoying a drink with his golfing pal when a man in golf gear came in, holding a white stick and being led by a guide dog.

'That guy's amazing,' said the punter's pal. 'Blind as a bat but he still plays golf – he's just gone round in ninety-five.'

'No!' said the incredulous punter. 'I must have a chat with him.'

The two got talking and soon discovered they shared a love of gambling.

'Perhaps we could play a round for a small wager?' said the blind player.

'Well, yes, but it wouldn't be fair, I wouldn't like to take your money off you. Maybe we could play for a fiver.'

'A fiver? What are you, man or mouse?' asked the blind golfer. 'I never play for less than £500.'

'Okay, right, if you insist,' said the punter, becoming irritated. 'But let's make it for £1000.'

'Right,' said the blind man.

'That's settled then, the game's on. We'll play tomorrow, right, what time?'

'Midnight,' said the blind man.

The racecourse bookie found an unopened pay packet, accidentally dropped by a racegoer.

He picked up the pay packet, opened it and groaned.

'What's the matter, mate, you must have had a right result there,' said the bookie's colleague.

'A result! You should see the bloody tax the bastards have stopped me.'

With form lines reading P (Pulled Up), R (Refused), U (Unseated Rider) and F (Fell) it was little surprise that the horse started at no-hoper odds of 100/1, but as it jumped the last and drew away to a shock victory an Irish punter was observed shouting and cheering.

'T'be sure, and Oi had all me wages on the nag.'

'How come?' asked a baffled punter.

'Well, an' didn't yer horse have de best form in de race? Promising, Ran well, Unlucky loser and Fit and fancied.'

The punter's creed: 'You don't gamble to win – you gamble so you can gamble the next day.'

As one gambler said to another: 'I hope I break even tonight, I could do with the money.'

At a race meeting many years ago, long before the photo finish had been invented, a huge 'coup' was planned on a horse which just couldn't lose.

The horse's connections all travelled to the track and

plunged fortunes on the horse, which started a hot favourite.

The race was run, and in a close finish the 'good thing' just held off a determined challenge by a 20/1 outsider to win by half a length.

So the horse's connections were dismayed to see the 20/1 outsider's number go up in the frame as the winner.

Outraged, they rushed to argue with the judge. Even the chief steward had backed the 'good thing' and he said to the Judge, 'That was pretty close, surely the favourite just held on?'

'Yes, wasn't it close. Do you know that 20/1 shot is the first winner I've backed for weeks.'

Then there was the compulsive gambler who was chucked out of Gamblers Anonymous for trying to bet on how long it would take him to give it up.

The soccer manager had finally given up hope of reforming his star player, a compulsive gambler.

'If only he could pass a betting shop like he passes a football,' he groaned.

The famous TV compere, presenter of 'What's My Line?' was enjoying a day at the races when he decided to put £500 on a horse.

He walked up to a bookie with his money. The bookie told him he would only accept £50 of the bet.

'Do you know who I am?' asked the compere.

'Course I do, mate, you're the compere of that "What's My

Line?" – A great programme.'

'How would you like to be on it?'

'Yeah, great.'

'You'll do well – nobody will ever guess you're supposed to be a bloody bookmaker.'

I t was the punter's sixty-sixth birthday on June 6, the sixth day of the sixth month in 1966.

Checking the racing pages he noticed that in the sixth race horse number six was called Lucky Six, and quoted at 6/1.

He rushed to the bookies to put £6 on it.

It finished sixth.

S tudying his race card, the punter asked the bookie, 'What do I get if Rubber wins at 10/1, Elastic at 11/1 and Springy at 12/1?'

'A cheque that bounces.'

T he trainer was preparing his horse for the race and, as the jockey mounted, the trainer told him: 'I've run out of patience with this bugger. If he doesn't produce the goods today I'm going to flog him to the local dairy to pull milk carts!'

The race began and the horse was beginning to lose ground so the jockey began to whip him along. Suddenly the horse shouted to the jockey, 'Go easy on me, mate, I've got to be up early in the morning!'

The gambler finally pulled off the roulette win of a lifetime – he calculated that his bets on number eighteen in various combinations would net him £150,000.

However, the casino manager came across to tell the gambler that the house limit was £100,000.

'That's not fair,' declared the gambler. 'Give me my money back at once.'

The apprentice jockey was preparing for his first ever ride and asked the trainer whether he had a chance of winning.

'Are you kidding? I've put a monkey on it and the wife's got a pony on it.'

'Oh – so where am I going to sit?'

The bookie and his tic-tac man were half way through a meeting when the tic-tac man suffered a heart attack and dropped dead.

'How am I going to break this to his wife?' thought the bookie as he rang her with the bad news. As she answered the bookie said, 'I'm afraid your husband has just died.'

'He hasn't!' she gasped.

'Wanna bet?'

Three racehorses walked into a public bar together, ordered three pints and stood chatting. One of them asked his mates whether they had been racing recently.

'Yes,' replied the grey horse. 'I ran at Doncaster on Saturday and, do you know, I was ten lengths behind the leader with two furlongs to go when I felt a ruddy great needle stuck in

my behind – well, I nearly took off. I've never moved so fast. Anyway, I won by a neck at 14/1.'

'Well, I never,' said the black horse, 'I ran at Pontefract three weeks ago and I was tailed off with half a mile to go when I felt a needle up my rump – boy, did I shift! My jockey could hardly pull me up after the race. I won by three lengths at 20/1.'

'Funny you should both tell me that,' said the third horse, a chestnut, 'because I wondered whether that had happened to you too. When I was running in a hurdle race at Catterick on Friday I felt a needle in my behind – well, after that I could have jumped Becher's Brook. I won by ten lengths at 12/1.'

Just then a greyhound sitting in the corner with his pint interrupted their conversation.

'Excuse me,' he said, 'I couldn't help but hear your conversation. I ran at Wimbledon last Tuesday and at the second bend I was well behind when all of a sudden someone chucked something at me from the crowd. I felt this needle go into my behind and I flew round the last two bends and won by a short head!'

'Well, would you believe it?' said the grey, black and chestnut racehorses together. 'A bloody talking greyhound!'

L ester Piggott's mount in the big race was beaten by a short head. As he dismounted from the horse, Lester was punched in the nose by an angry punter who had lost money by betting on him.

In court later the punter said that his twin brother, who had also backed the horse, had volunteered to carry out the attack on Lester, but that he always preferred to stick it on the nose rather than rely on cross doubles.

Punters and betting-shop staff watched in astonishment as a scruffy-looking individual walked through the door waving his arms about and calling to someone outside: 'That's it, gently does it, bring her in now.' As he continued to call and wave the rear quarters of a horse appeared in the doorway, followed slowly by the back of the horse and then, finally, its head.

'What the bloody hell do you think you're doing?' yelled the shop manager at the scruffy individual who looked at him calmly and said, 'Oh, I didn't think you'd mind, the bloke outside said anyone could back a horse in here.'

The angling contest was under orders when the punter rushed up to back Bert Smith to make the largest catch at odds of 10/1.

Bert fished brilliantly and his 26 lb plaice was duly judged to be the heaviest catch of the day.

Jubilantly, the punter dashed off to find the bookie who handed over a couple of notes to the lucky winner.

'Here, what's this, you've only paid me out at 2/1 instead of 10/1,' complained the punter.

'Read the rules, mate,' said the bookie. 'We always bet a fifth the odds a plaice.'

The jockey came in for a spare ride on a horse he'd never come across before.

'He's a bloody great jumper – the only thing is, you must remember as you come to the fences to call one, two, UP just as you want him to take off,' instructed the trainer.

The race began, the runners came to the first fence, but in all the hurly-burly of the race the jockey forgot the 'one,

two, UP' and his horse ploughed through the fence, almost crashing to the ground, and really shaking up the jockey.

'I'd better do what the trainer told me,' he thought. And as they came to the next he duly called 'one, two, UP' and the horse soared over the fence like a stag.

He didn't forget again, the horse jumped superbly and they won by twenty lengths.

Back in the winner's enclosure the jockey asked the trainer, 'What's all that about, the "one, two, UP"?'

'Oh, I must have forgotten to mention – the horse is blind.'

The French jockey who had ridden the Derby winner had been invited to attend a grand Ball to celebrate and asked to say a few words. He spoke no English at all, though, and asked a colleague to jot him down a couple of lines which he would read out parrot fashion.

He duly arrived at the function with his notes, was introduced and stood up to speak: 'Ladeez and gennellmen, I em fuckin' glad to be 'ere wiz all you wankers . . .'

The jockey in the two-horse race was asked what he thought of his chances.

'Well, whatever beats me will win the bloody race.'

The punter strode up to the bookie and asked for a bet of £500 on the 10/1 outsider in the field of three runners. The bookie took the bet, rubbed out the 10/1 and chalked up 12/1. Back came the punter with another £500 which the bookie took, rubbed off 12/1 and chalked up 14/1.

The punter came back – another £500 – out went the odds to 66/1.

'Excuse me asking,' said the punter, 'but why do you keep knocking the odds out every time I back that horse?'

'Well, now you've had your bets I'll let you into a little secret – I happen to know that horse can't win. You see, I own it.'

'Oh,' said the punter. 'Well, this is going to be a bloody funny race – I own the other two.'

There was one race to go, the racegoer had backed a couple of winners and enjoyed more than a few glasses of champers to celebrate. He suddenly realized that the runners were coming to the last fence in the last race of the day so he rushed to the top step of the Grandstand to get a better view.

Slightly the worse for wear, he missed his footing and tumbled back down the steps, falling heavily, cutting his head as he went and taking a number of innocent bystanders with him.

Waking up the next morning in hospital, he began to come round slowly and remember what had happened.

In the bed next to him, with his leg hoisted up in the air and plastered from ankle to thigh, was an elderly gentleman.

'And what happened to you?' asked the racegoer.

'You'll never believe it, but I was at the races yesterday and was up in the Grandstand watching the last race when some bloody drunk fell down the steps and took half the stand with him. What happened to you?'

The night before the Grand National a young couple were discovered on the course making love by Becher's Brook. They were arrested for offending public decency.

When they appeared in court the next morning they asked for ten other fences to be taken into consideration.

The apprentice jockey was hauled up before the stewards to explain his riding of the hot favourite which had failed to win.

'What instructions did the trainer give you?' demanded the chief steward.

'I was told to wait,' said the jockey.

'Until when?' barked the steward.

'Until Saturday week at Newmarket, sir.'

A ventriloquist on holiday in Newmarket came across a large stud farm. He asked for a tour of the place and was escorted around by one of the stable lads.

As he was shown the highly valuable stallions and their partners the ventriloquist began to make the horses 'talk'.

Startled, the lad raced off to tell his boss what was happening, shouting, 'The horses are talking – but if any one of them says anything about me, they're lying!'

A jockeys' team were playing the local cricket side in a match, but they were one player short until a local trainer offered them the services of one of his horses.

'Can he bowl?' asked the jockeys' skipper, doubtfully.

'Of course, just stick the ball in his hoof,' said the trainer.

They put him on to bowl and he promptly took six wickets

in his first over and finished the local side off in his second.

'Can he bat?' asked the jockeys' skipper.

'Of course – just put the bat between his front hooves.'

In went the padded-up horse to open the batting. He hit the first ball firmly towards the boundary.

'Run,' shouted the jockeys' skipper beginning to advance down the wicket.

'Run?' said the trainer. 'Don't be stupid – if he could bloody well run I'd have entered him for the Derby.'

A woman spotted her punter husband poring over the racing pages of the newspaper: 'I don't know why you're wasting your time trying to find the winners – they'll all be listed in the *Sporting Life* tomorrow.'

The wealthy gambler was on his way into the plush casino when he was accosted by a scruffy, dirty tramp:

'Spare the cash for a cup of tea, guv?'

Touched by the tramp's plight, the punter said:

'I'll do better than that, come in with me and have a large scotch.'

'Sorry, sir, I don't drink.'

'Well, then – here's one of my finest Havana cigars.'

'Sorry, sir, I don't smoke.'

'Oh. Well, listen, I've been given a "good thing" for Ascot tomorrow. Put every penny you can beg on it and here's a fiver to start the ball rolling.'

'Sorry, sir, I don't gamble. All I want is a cup of tea.'

'And you shall have it. Come on, we're going straight to my home – I want my wife to see for herself just what happens to a man who doesn't drink, smoke or gamble!'

Watching the horses parading before the race, spectators were astonished to see one of the runners plodding round wearing four brown boots, one on each foot.

One of the bemused racegoers asked the trainer, 'Why is your horse wearing brown boots?'

'Because his black ones are at the cobbler's.'

The inveterate punter was on his way home after another losing session. He didn't even have the fare home so he thumbed a lift.

A Rolls-Royce stopped for him and he jumped into the chauffeur-driven car, whose wealthy occupant listened to the punter's tale of woe before delivering him a lecture on the evils of gambling and giving him £50 which he made him promise to hand straight over to his wife for housekeeping.

A couple of weeks later the same punter was on his way home again, once again he didn't have two pennies to rub together. Again he was thumbing and again the Rolls-Royce came along and gave him a lift.

This time the wealthy man was even more irate when the punter admitted he had strayed off the straight and narrow.

'Here's £50, take it straight home to your wife – and don't make the same mistake again.'

He might as well have saved his breath. A few days later, on his way past Sandown racecourse the wealthy businessman spotted the punter thumbing a lift home. He told his chauffeur to slow down and as he pulled alongside the man he wound the window down to talk to him.

As soon as the punter spotted the Rolls he broke into a trot and began to run away.

'Keep away from me!' he shouted. 'You're a jinx – every time you give me a lift I lose me money!'

'You'll get round safely enough on this one, it can jump houses,' the trainer told the jockey just before the start of the race.

The horse fell at the first fence.

'What happened?' the trainer asked the returning jockey.

'He must have tripped over the bloody chimney!'

Two astrologers were discussing a third astrologer who they had spotted in a casino.

'He's betting as though there was no tomorrow,' said one.

'Do you think he knows something?' replied the other.

Two trainers in conversation: 'I call my owners mushrooms.'

'Why's that?'

'Because I like to keep them in the dark and feed them heaps of shit.'

Two punters discussing the outcome of a race:

'That horse I just backed must be bloody good.'

'Why's that then – it lost!'

'Yes, but it took twenty other horses to beat it.'

The trainer had a large bet on his horse, but it lost. He asked the jockey:

'Was the going too soft?'

'The going was no problem – it was the coming back which beat us!'

The stable lad was new at the racing game and when the local steward at the racecourse asked him about his horse's pedigree he was lost for words.

'What do you mean by pedigree?'

'I mean, what is he by and what is he out of?'

'He's by himself and he's outside the door!'

The police watched the horse box come hammering down the road at least thirty miles faster than the speed limit.

They chased it and made it pull over, got out and walked over to the driver.

'Where are you going in such a hurry, sir?'

'I've got to get to the races – I'm a stable lad for a big trainer.'

The policemen walked around to the back of the horse box to take a look inside.

It was empty.

'There are no horses in your horse box, sir.'

'No, of course there aren't, I'm taking the non-runners.'

Paddy, not the brightest of punters, was celebrating backing a 100/1 winner.

One of his mates asked him how he'd picked the horse out.

''Twas obvious, the first thing I spotted when I arrived at the races was a number seven on the bookies' stand – then I saw a big advertising banner with a number seven on it, then I noticed the seven furlong post.'

'But your horse wasn't number seven,' said his mate.

'That's where I was clever – I'd seen three sevens, and I said to myself, three sevens are twenty-two, so I backed number 22 and it bolted in!'

The bookie asked the old lady how she regularly backed a winner a day. 'I stick a pin in the paper,' she said.

Next day she backed a winning treble and again the bookie asked her how she'd done it. 'I couldn't find a pin, so I used a fork,' she said.

Three bookies gathered round the grave of a recently deceased punter.

The first bookie, conscience stricken after the bereavement, looked down at the coffin and said: 'He'd just backed a winner for twenty quid with me.' And he dropped four fivers into the grave.

The second bookie looked down and said: 'I'd just laid him four fivers about a winner, too.' And he put two tenners on to the coffin.

The third bookie said: 'He must have been on a winning streak, I owed him a score, too.' And he took out his cheque book, wrote out a cheque for £60, dropped it into the grave and pocketed the £40 cash!

Four jockeys were killed in a car crash. Their wives arrived to identify the bodies.

Without hesitation one of the wives made straight for the fourth coffin and said, even before it had been opened, 'That's my husband.'

'How do you know?' said the police.

'He was never in the first three in his life – and it's too late for him to change now.'

Jack Logan of the *Sporting Life* told this story:
An Irish priest told me about a lady punter who always went to confession with a list of sins carefully written out to make sure that none had been overlooked.

'Father,' she said, starting on the list in front of her, '£5 to win Forgive 'n' Forget, £2 each way The Thinker . . .'

Suddenly she realized her mistake.

'Oh, Father,' she cried, 'I've left my sins in Ladbrokes.'

As the horses jumped the last the leading jockey suddenly found himself being pelted with tomatoes, apples, eggs, pickled onions, gherkins, even a bottle of champers.

At the stewards' enquiry he was asked what had happened: 'Couldn't you see I was bloody well hampered,' he replied.

The two drinkers were gloomily discussing their gambling mad wives.

'I wish I'd never got married,' said the first. 'She's bingo mad – it's all she talks about – even in bed.'

'Think yourself lucky,' said the second drinker. 'My wife's crazy about one-armed bandits. Every morning I wake up with a sore tool and a mouthful of 50p pieces.'

The Irish priest was bequeathed a donkey by a deceased parishioner.

Father Murphy soon discovered that the donkey was a very fast runner. Thinking he might win some money for parish funds he entered the donkey for a race. Parishioners rushed to bet on the donkey, which came in third.

The local paper ran a story: 'Father Murphy's Ass Shows'.

The Archbishop saw the paper and was not amused but by then the priest had entered the donkey for another race, which it won.

The paper's headline announced: 'Father Murphy's Ass Out In Front'.

The Archbishop immediately banned the priest from running the donkey in any more races. The paper reported: 'Archbishop Scratches Father Murphy's Ass'.

'Sell the donkey, or get rid of it,' demanded the Archbishop. So the priest reluctantly gave it away to a nun he knew. 'Father Murphy Gives His Ass to Sister Agatha', trumpeted the paper.

By now, the Archbishop was being driven to distraction and demanded that the nun dispose of the donkey. She sold it for £10.

'Sister Agatha Sells Her Ass for £10', ran the headline.

The Archbishop went out and got drunk!

The keen punter set off on a round the world trip.

In Switzerland he won a parrot in a pub raffle. Like most Swiss, the parrot was multi-lingual. It could speak three languages fluently.

Realizing the parrot's potential as a betting medium the punter quickly caught a plane back to London and took the parrot with him to the races.

Placing the parrot on the racecourse bar the punter offered to bet £100 that it could converse in English, German or French.

The bet was quickly covered and the gambler asked the parrot: 'Sprechen Sie Deutsch?'

Silence. Not a peep. Not a squawk.

The punter paid up and took the parrot away. When he got home he said to it, 'I've a good mind to strangle you, you let me down badly.'

'Don't be stupid,' said the parrot, 'think of the odds we'll get tomorrow.'

A crooked trainer sold off a useless old horse which he knew wouldn't see out the week to another trainer, who seemed quite happy to buy it.

Eventually curiosity got the better of the first trainer, who just had to find out why the other had bought the broken down old nag.

'Er, how's that horse I sold you the other day?' asked the first trainer upon meeting the other at the races.

'Oh, he died the day after I bought him from you.'

'I'm sorry to hear that,' said the first.

'Not to worry,' said the second. 'I raffled him and sold over a thousand tickets at two quid a go.'

'But what did the winner say when he found out the horse had died?'

'Well, he wasn't too happy at first – but I gave him his two quid back.'

Just before the 'off' of the big race the chief steward spotted the trainer giving his horse something.

'What was that, trainer?' asked the steward.

'Oh, just a harmless lump of sugar. Look, I'll eat some myself.'

Not convinced, the steward asked to try a lump of the sugar for himself.

As the jockey prepared to load the horse into the stalls the trainer whispered to him, 'Go straight to the front and stay there. It's a certainty, you can't get beat. And don't worry if you hear something coming up behind you – it'll only be me or the chief steward!'

Strip poker is probably the only game in which the more you lose the more you have to show for it.

'Stop cheating!' the dealer told the card player.

'I'm not!' claimed the player.

'You must be,' said the dealer, 'that's not the hand I dealt you.'

'My horse loves a gamble,' the jockey told a colleague. 'Every time we come to a fence he tosses me for it.'

An Irish priest was interviewed by journalists at the 1982 Cheltenham Festival race meeting. He asked the journalists to grant him anonymity. 'I have told my Bishop that I am on a course,' he said. 'But he may not be happy if he discovers that I meant a race course.'

The novice croupier had just started his first job at the casino. His boss greeted him on his first night. 'You're going to like it here, we're a friendly bunch. After work on a Wednesday night we all get together and go to a drinking club and get drunk until we're sick as pigs and fall over. You'll love it.'

'Well, no,' said the croupier, 'I don't really approve of drinking.'

'Oh, well, on Thursday night after the casino closes we go to an illegal gambling club I know and play poker until dawn.'

'Ah,' said the croupier, 'I work hard to earn my money. I have no wish to gamble it away.'

'Oh, well, on Friday night after the casino closes we get a bunch of girls in from the strip club over the road and . . .'

'Well, no,' says the croupier, 'actually I've never really been into that sort of thing.'

'What! You're not gay are you?'

'Well, no.'

'Oh, then you certainly won't enjoy Saturday nights . . .'

TRUE? YOU BET

Brough Scott once said during a race commentary: 'And there's the unmistakable figure of Joe Mercer . . . or is it Lester Piggott?'

During a televised race meeting, David Coleman told viewers: 'That's the magic of television, I've just been told over the headphones who finished third.'

And one Grand National day, Coleman informed viewers: 'And in 1900 the owner of the Grand National winner was the then Prince of Wales, King Edward VII.'

Viewers were bemused when racing pundit Jimmy Lindley pointed out: 'These two horses have met five times this season, and I think they've beaten each other on each occasion.'

Racing writer, Chris Poole, explained to readers: 'A racehorse is not like a machine. It has to be tuned up, just like you tune up a racing motor car.'

'What are your immediate thoughts?' Brough Scott asked jockey Walter Swinburn, who replied: 'I don't have any immediate thoughts at the moment.'

The hustler was taking the mug punter to the cleaners during a game of poker.
The hustler called for a short break in play while he went to the gents.
'Will you excuse me?' he asked the mug punter.
'Certainly. For the first time today I'll know what you have in your hand.'

Little Johnny had a gambling problem.
His worried parents and his teacher got together to discuss it.

'What he really needs is the shock of losing a large amount of pocket money – that will bring him to his senses,' said the teacher. 'I'll wait for the right opportunity and try to arrange it.'

Next day, little Johnny was, as usual, persuading classmates to bet with him in the playground. His teacher heard him whispering to a pal, 'I bet I know what colour knickers Miss is wearing.'

Seeing her opportunity, teacher pounced.

'Ah, Johnny, so you think you know what colour knickers I'm wearing? I bet you five pounds you don't.'

'Please, Miss,' said Johnny. 'They're red, Miss.'

Teacher lifted her dress to reveal blue underwear.

'Now, hand over the five pounds, Johnny, and let that be a lesson – it doesn't pay to gamble.'

Triumphantly, teacher rang Johnny's father. 'It worked, I think we've finally cured him. I overheard him telling a classmate in the playground that he knew what colour knickers I had on, so I bet him a fiver he didn't, showed him he was wrong, and took the money from him – that should be the end of his gambling.'

Replied the father gloomily, 'I don't think so – before he left for school this morning Johnny bet me £10 he could get you to lift up your dress in the playground and show off your knickers!'

Joe had frequented the same betting shop for a quarter of a century, yet he'd never managed to show a profit on a day's gambling.

When the betting shop's head office heard about this they decided to name Joe the country's unluckiest punter

and to hold a small ceremony at which they would offer him a free bet to make up for his disappointments over the years.

Having called a press conference, the shop company's PR man announced that he was going to tear a betting slip into ten pieces and write a different amount on each, from £10 to £100 each. These would be put into the company MD's bowler hat and Joe would draw one of them out, winning the appropriate free bet.

With flash bulbs popping Joe put his hand into the hat to draw out his free bet.

'Well, which have you drawn out?' asked the PR man.

Joe replied, '6⅞!'

The unlucky punters had lost on five consecutive races. With just one event remaining one punter said to the other: 'That priest over there – he's been making a sign over one horse in each race, then backing it, and he's had five winners.'

The punters decided to watch the priest closely and back the horse over which he made the sign this time with all their remaining cash.

Sure enough, he made the sign, they backed the horse and it dashed into a clear lead in the race when, with only yards to run, it collapsed and died.

Devastated, the punters went over and spoke to the priest, explaining that they had decided to back the horse because he had made a sign over it.

Said the priest: 'That's the trouble with you atheists. You can't tell the difference between a blessing and the last rites.'

Interviewed after a race run on very heavy going, the jockey told the TV man: 'I was trotting up to the start when I saw a jockey's cap on the ground and I leaned down to pick it up. Just as I grabbed the cap I heard a voice say, "Don't pull until I get my feet out of the stirrups"!'

A keen gambling man on holiday in Italy is passing the Vatican. He decides to pop in to see the Pope, but is told by an aide that His Holiness is unavailable.

He tries on three consecutive days, getting the same answer. On the final attempt the aide tells the man: 'Sadly, the Pope has passed on – that's of course why you can't see him, but we do not wish to release this news to the world just yet, so we would appreciate it if you would say nothing.'

The man returns home and rushes straight to his local bookmaker and gets odds of 100/1 against the Pope dying before the end of the week.

On his way out of the bookies the punter sees an old man sobbing his heart out.

'What's the matter?' he asks.

The man tells him he has lost everything and cannot afford to pay his bills.

'Listen, don't tell anyone else, but I've got a certainty for you. I'll lend you a tenner – put it on the Pope being announced dead by the end of the week.'

Sure enough, the announcement of the Pope's demise is made, and the man goes to the betting shop to collect his winnings. On the way out he meets the old man again, but he is still sobbing his heart out.

'What's the matter? You must have won a fortune. Didn't you put the bet on?'

'Yes, I did,' said the old man, 'but I doubled up the Pope with the Archbishop of Canterbury.'

The racehorse owner had to admit that the latest nag he'd bought was useless, after it came in last ten times on the trot. He decided to sell it at auction.

The only bid which came in for the horse was for £10.

Raising the hammer on the rostrum, the auctioneer turned to the owner:

'Should I knock him down, sir?'

'Only as a last resort,' said the owner. 'Sell him if you can.'

The keen punter was about to enter Ascot racecourse when a funeral passed by.

The punter stopped, removed his hat and placed it over his heart, head bowed.

His friends were very impressed at this touching scene and told the punter so.

'Well, it was the least I could do, she was always a good wife to me. Had one big fault, though – hated horse racing.'

The wife was used to her old man coming home in the early hours after his regular weekly poker school.

But this week he seemed to be making a hell of a lot more noise than usual. She could hear him shouting out, 'Get up and get your bags packed you old cow!'

Waking up in a fury she shouted at him, 'What the bloody hell do you mean?'

'I mean bloody well get up and get packed, you're leaving. I lost you in the poker game.'

'How in the name of Heaven could you possibly lose me in a game of cards?' she demanded.

'It wasn't bloody easy, I had to chuck in four aces – now bloody well get up and get packed!'

Three men were sitting in a bar arguing about which of them had the largest manhood.

They finally agreed that the only way to settle the matter was to strike a three-way bet for £100 each and then whip out their equipment to rest on the bar to be judged by the barman.

The money was handed over to the barman then all three whipped out their willies and sat them on the bar.

The barman was looking and scratching his head when in walked an effeminate-looking customer.

'Yes, sir, may I help you?' asked the barman.

'Mm, well, I did come in for a cocktail,' lisped the limp-wristed customer. 'But looking at what you have on show I think I'll try one of your bar snacks.'

S howbiz tycoon Lord Bernard Delfont was a keen race-horse owner, but he finally decided the time had come to quit the sport when his trainer told him one of his horses was crazy.

'When a jumper I had wouldn't take a fence, the trainer seriously told me the horse would need psychiatric treatment. I knew that was enough and got out.'